SMART PERSONAL MONEY CREDIT

HOW TO AVOID BAD CREDIT TRAPS AND LOW CREDIT SCORES

DC JAMES

TABLE OF CONTENTS

The Smart Money Finance Checklist — v
Introduction — vii

1. Understanding Smart Personal Money Credit — 1
2. Personal Credit and Business Funding — 2
3. What is Credit? — 3
4. Applying for Credit — 4
5. A Damaged Credit Report — 5
6. Here is Why Credit is Very Important — 6
7. Bad Credit and What Can Happen to Someone's Life — 7
8. Having Bad Credit is Bad — 8
9. Here is How Much a Person Can Pay With Having Bad Credit — 9
10. Homes Can Cost Much More For Someone With Bad Credit — 10
11. Credit Cards Cost More For A Person With Bad Credit — 11
12. Bad Credit Controls People's Lives — 12
13. The Bad Credit Trap and Why it is So Awful — 13
14. Things Happen to People All The Time — 15
15. Life When Someone Has Good Credit — 16
16. Issuing Credit Lines — 17
17. Good Credit is The Secret — 18
18. Your Role in The Credit System — 19
19. Applying For Credit — 20
20. Revealing Credit Score — 21
21. Breaking Down The Credit Score — 22
22. Running Into Problems With Credit — 26
23. Taking On Extra Work — 27
24. Good Credit is The Way To Go — 28
25. Accumulating Debt Over Time — 29

26. Living Within Your Means	30
27. A Word On Budgets	31
Leave a One Click Review	33
CONCLUSION	35
About the Author	37

© 2020 Copyright Red E. Wrighter Books LLC, DC JAMES - **All rights reserved.**

The content contained within this book may not be reproduced, duplicated or transmitted without direct written permission from the author or the publisher.

Under no circumstances will any blame or legal responsibility be held against the publisher, or author, for any damages, reparation, or monetary loss due to the information contained within this book. Either directly or indirectly, you are responsible for your own choices, actions, and results.

Legal Notice:

This book is copyright protected. This book is only for personal use. You cannot amend, distribute, sell, use, quote or paraphrase any part, or the content within this book, without the consent of the author or publisher.

Disclaimer Notice:

Please note the information contained within this document is for educational and entertainment purposes only. All effort has been executed to present accurate, up to date, and reliable, complete information. No warranties of any kind are declared or implied. Readers acknowledge that the author is not engaging in the rendering of legal, financial, medical or professional advice. The content within this book has been derived from various sources. Please consult a licensed professional before attempting any techniques outlined in this book.

By reading this document, the reader agrees that under no circumstances is the author responsible for any losses, direct or indirect, which are incurred as a result of the use of the information contained within this document, including, but not limited to, — errors, omissions, or inaccuracies.

INTRODUCTION

SMART PERSONAL MONEY CREDIT gives entrepreneurs a unique opportunity to build, maintain and get credit, both individually and for business purposes.

Why do you want to get out of debt? Is it because you want to feel more in control of your financial life? Is it because it frustrates you living from paycheck to paycheck? Is it because you want to improve your credit score so you can get better loan and mortgage terms? Is it because you want to cultivate a better relationship with money or to get started on the path to financial freedom?

To win over debt, the motive behind your goal has to be a personal 'must'. If the factors driving your desire to take control of your finances are not personal imperatives attached with the committed desire to change your situation, you are unlikely to take the actions necessary to create financial stability that will cause a life of abundance.

Take a moment to think about why you want to get out of debt. On the surface, getting out of debt will improve your life in so many ways. Perhaps, at a minimum, you want to get out of debt so you manage how much you earn and how much you spend to allocate your money from one month to the next depending on your financial goals and aims.

Perhaps you want to get out of debt so you can have peace of mind each month in knowing that you have enough money to cover your basic needs and still have enough funds left over to save, invest, and maybe indulge a habit. Perhaps you want to get out of debt so you can get started on saving towards your dream home, wedding, vacation, car, experience, etc.

Make sure that the factors driving your desire to become debt free and financially stable are well-defined and personal must haves because getting out of debt can often be arduous and challenging depending on your present debt level and financial state. The stronger your WHY, the more the likelihood of sticking with the process and from it, yields significant results!

Now that you have pinpointed your ultimate reason for wanting to get out of debt, gain more control over your finances, and get started on the path to financial freedom, you need to understand something of crucial importance:

Depending on how much you earn each month and the different expense allocation buckets your income has to fill each month, you'll know that it is possible to live a completely debt free life. Ultimately, all you really need to do is: live within your means—spend less than you earn—save, and invest in profitable ventures. The more consistently you can do this, the faster you will realize financial success.

The word debt often has negative connotations attached to it. While often seen as negative, debt is not always bad; you can also have what they call 'good debt.' Establishing a distinction between the two is important. A poor credit score is often a result of bad debt, or rather, excessive spending on depreciating assets (i.e. assets that lose their value with use or over time).

For instance, using your credit card to shop for clothes, services, electronics, travel and other items that satisfy your immediate desires is bad debt because what you are doing is buying things that will neither generate income nor appreciate in value (e.g. assets).

When you borrow money to invest in appreciating assets such as a business, your education, a house, your self-betterment. You are getting into good debt; good debt is any money borrowed and directed towards income generating ventures of any nature.

One key thing to note about good debt is that getting it normally requires good credit. This means if you have bad credit, accruing any form of debt, including good debt, will be problematic because your credit score is the primary factor lenders look at when determining whether you are credit worthy—capable of repaying the debt—and the interest to affix to the debt.

Since both debts can take many shapes and forms, determining whether a debt is good or bad boils down to your present financial life and aims. You should always aim to accrue good debt and to avoid (or minimize) bad debt at all costs. If you have already accrued some bad debts, know that they are affecting your credit score negatively, and therefore take immediate action to rectify the matter by creating an effective debt free plan.

Since bad debt is the primary cause of bad credit, let's talk more about bad credit.

The ultimate definition of a poor credit score or "bad credit" is "a displayed failure to keep up with your financial obligations." Simplified, having poor credit means you have shown a tendency to borrow money and not keep up with the repayments as promised.

When your credit is poor, because you have displayed a failure to keep up with your payments, lenders and creditors will not trust you and therefore deny you any future loans.

Creditors use your credit score to determine whether to grant you a loan. When your score is poor, it tells a lender you have shown a tendency not to keep up with your financial obligations. What lender would willingly lend money to someone who has shown a clear history of not repaying his or her debts?

Your credit score also affects your mortgage rate. When your credit score is poor, you are likely to pay a higher mortgage rate—if you are lucky enough to find a willing lender; the higher your credit score (740+), the more attractive you are to lenders and the less you are likely to pay more in interest for conventional loans such as mortgages.

Poor credit also influences the interest rate you pay when you get a loan. Most often, a bad credit score results in higher interest rates—on everything including credit cards, mortgage, car loans, insurance, etc., while a good credit score means favorable interest rates.

A poor credit score has many negative effects on your life, which is why you must commit to repaying your debt as effectively as so you can boldly walk the path to financial stability and freedom.

Ideally you have identified a powerful reason for wanting to get out and stay out of debt, you know about good and bad debt, and you know about how bad debt and a bad credit score affects different areas of your life.

With this book in your hands, you are about to become a smart personal money credit master. You will know exactly how to build and keep a smart personal money credit profile. With this personal credit profile built, you can get large amounts of credit and funding.

And now this book will give you the knowledge and power to fight and win the smart personal money credit battle.

1

UNDERSTANDING SMART PERSONAL MONEY CREDIT

Understanding personal money credit is very important. It not only matters for a person when they want to purchase something with an outrageous amount of money, but it is also important for business credit.

Making sure that you understand how your personal credit will affect your affairs of life is something that you need to know about. It can be necessary when applying for funding, and or managing your business for many things from buildings to equipment.

2

PERSONAL CREDIT AND BUSINESS FUNDING

Keep in mind that there are a lot of business credit sources that will approve for business funding without a personal credit check. When this happens, a business will use credit like American Express, MasterCard, Visa, and store cards. But, when applying for loans, credit lines, and more, there will be a credit check that will come from the lender.

They will most likely decide based on one not using their personal credit as a red flag and that the business owner is having problems with their financial life. That is why it is important to keep your personal credit in good standing.

3

WHAT IS CREDIT?

You need to understand how credit works. It is an agreement between the creditor or a lender of some sort (there are many of them) and the borrower. The borrower is assuming something of value with this agreement.

They will need to pay the creditor back, and it has certain terms that must follow strict terms and conditions. This is typical of what car dealers, banks, and other creditors do regularly. They extend credit to individuals that want to purchase something.

APPLYING FOR CREDIT

When you apply for credit, they will check your credit profile or report seeing if you can pay the debt. The lender will decide on whether to extend the credit to the person. Therefore, it is so important to keep your credit report good because it ups your consumer score and you will receive better terms on the lending.

A DAMAGED CREDIT REPORT

Sometimes, a person will have a damaged credit report and lenders will give them the credit, but at a higher interest rate. These rates will vary, but they can be very high. In the year 2009, during the time of the signing of the Credit Card Act with so-called "unfair or deceptive practices" one credit card had an APR of 89%. This is high and you don't want to fall into this category, so keeping your credit in good standing is very important.

HERE IS WHY CREDIT IS VERY IMPORTANT

Your credit is part of your life. If they have denied you a loan or jobs because of your credit, then you know that it is important. Everyone is affected by their credit when they pay car payments, home loans, rent, credit cards, installment loans, cell phones, insurance, and utilities. These are all based on the personal credit that a person has. It is impossible for someone to hide from his or her credit.

Lenders, Underwriters are looking to make solid decisions on a person, to be sure that they will pay the bills or complete the jobs the market hires them for. This can make a tremendous difference in someone's life, and keeping a good credit score can make a difference in the quality of life that a person leads.

BAD CREDIT AND WHAT CAN HAPPEN TO SOMEONE'S LIFE

When there are credit issues that a person is experiencing, it may cost them a tremendous amount of money to just live. Most people do not have money to save up for emergencies because they are paying so much in interest charges. This causes them to live in a way that they may run into hard times much easier.

8

HAVING BAD CREDIT IS BAD

Since living life to the fullest and struggling all the time to survive, based on the quality of your credit, having bad credit can ruin one's life. A car is a good example of this. Most people need one to get around for work, their families, and for other reasons. Most people need a car, and there are about 250 million car owners in the US alone.

They usually finance their cars and pay monthly payments until they pay the debt off. They give the car loans to customers based on their credit history. Since they will pull credit scores on a person, consumers will get a car loan based on it. If it is bad, they will not get the loan at all or they will pay a lot more.

HERE IS HOW MUCH A PERSON CAN PAY WITH HAVING BAD CREDIT

Good credit will get someone a better interest rate. Bad credit will make you pay more. A $20,000 loan with good credit is $322, and they base it on 5% interest for 72 months. For a certain $20,000 car loan with bad credit, it will be around $541 a month with a high interest rate for 60 months. It is the same car, but one is costing about 219 more dollars each month.

The person with excellent credit will pay $23,184 for their car. The one with the bad credit will pay $32,460. That is a vast difference of $9,276 and it is 46% more than the person with good credit is paying. They base these examples of interest rates common for a $20,000 car loan.

HOMES CAN COST MUCH MORE FOR SOMEONE WITH BAD CREDIT

For a $100,000 mortgage, a good credit consumer will be $577. The house will cost them $207,720 over 30 years. With bad credit, someone will pay $841 each month over the 30 years it will cost you $302,760. Having good credit will allow a person to pay $264 less per month and save $95,040 over the time of the loan. The person with the bad credit will pay $95,040 in interest for a $100,000 loan.

CREDIT CARDS COST MORE FOR A PERSON WITH BAD CREDIT

When people have bad credit, their credit cards could cost $116 more than a month based on their credit. When they have utility payments, insurance payments, and other expenses, they will also be more.

BAD CREDIT CONTROLS PEOPLE'S LIVES

For many people, they know that bad credit isn't a good thing and that it can affect their lives negatively. They might not realize that in reality, their bad credit is controlling their lives and it can really make an enormous difference. They will pay very high-interest rates and it will be difficult for them to live.

They won't be able to save for emergencies and they will always worry about paying the bills. For them, life will not be easy at all and they will wish that they had kept their credit in better standing so they could live a better life.

13

THE BAD CREDIT TRAP AND WHY IT IS SO AWFUL

It is a trap that most consumers will never get out of because they cannot recover from it financially. In my lifetime, I have heard many stories about how someone had superb credit and it went bad, but I never heard of one with bad credit that turned around to be good again. That is because most people with bad credit find it difficult to recover from it, and that is a fact.

The system is against them from the start, and the consumers with credit issues are not in their situations because of being bad people. They get sucked into a trap that they couldn't get out of. Many people develop credit problems from an uncontrollable event. It might be a car crash that leaves them with high medical bills. Other times, people go through a divorce that can cause their credit to go bad quickly when bills are overdue or not paid.

So many things can happen in life and when they do, people fall behind on their bills and they can't come back from it. Even one late bill from a credit card will cause even more problems. The creditors will lower their limits and the person's credit score always goes down. Based on 1/3 of the credit score that people receive on their available credit.

The consumer needs the credit, but it is not available and they will receive higher overdraft fees. Then the credit score drops and there are risks that can occur with other accounts that they might have.

14

THINGS HAPPEN TO PEOPLE ALL THE TIME

There are just so many things that can happen and when they do, accounts paid late and a downward credit spiral begins. Even when one payment is late for just one credit card, other companies will claim that the risk is higher. There will be an increase in interest rates. Sometimes, the creditors cannot do this but if it is in the fine print, they will be able to and this makes it so much more difficult for a consumer.

Once the interest rates go up, so do the payments and it now faces a person with the difficulty of handling many late bills at one time. These always have fees associated with them. Things can get bad in a short period. You now destroy the credit that was once good. It will complete any new credit approved at higher rates.

This can cost them so much money every month and their quality of life will deteriorate for many years to come. This is the BAD credit cycle and many times it starts with one late payment, but it costs many people a healthy financial future.

LIFE WHEN SOMEONE HAS GOOD CREDIT

Not all people can be rich, but they should strive to have good credit. Their quality of life depends on it. Mercedes Benz will sell someone a brand new car at around $351 a month when they have good credit which is great and a person can drive around in luxury. We can purchase even a magnificent home with good credit for less than $1,000 a month. Having good credit will open doors to good jobs and getting approved for credit at 0% interest.

16

ISSUING CREDIT LINES

A consumer will get their credit lines based on their credit quality. When they have good credit, they may receive a credit card with a $10,000 limit or even higher. This can allow them to buy the things they want and to use funds for emergencies that come up in their lives.

Treatment of clients with good credit are better than ones with bad credit by car dealers, banks, mortgage companies, and more. I don't agree that this should happen, but it does. And they give customers with good credit better deals than ones with bad credit.

Most times, good credit buyers are smart and educated and if they think they are not getting a good deal, they will leave. This gives many sales managers even more reasons to give good credit consumers the proper attention that they deserve.

Having good credit is like being rich. They treat you much better when you have it. You will spend more and live the life that you want.

GOOD CREDIT IS THE SECRET

The secret of life is having good credit. You will need to understand the credit system better, secrets behind your credit scores, and even the best and most proven ways to correct your credit.

YOUR ROLE IN THE CREDIT SYSTEM

People believe that there is someone watching out for them so that their credit report is correct and fair. Maybe they think the government is helping them with this, but this is not the truth. You are the only person responsible for your credit and who can enjoy your credit profile that's correct and positive. You are the one that can do this, so you need to understand your role in the credit system.

The credit bureaus have to follow state and federal laws. They also have to investigate whether there is a credit dispute. This is all under the Fair Credit Reporting Act. But to remember that the credit bureaus do not question what the creditors report about you unless you ask them to. The creditors also follow state and federal laws, but they do not have a department looking into that. They just want to make more money on your credit.

APPLYING FOR CREDIT

When you apply for new credit, they collect the data about your credit history. Once collected, they send it to the credit bureau for an inquiry. They send back a credit file that has all of your information in. This will list out past credit accounts, your credit score, home address, and employment information. The creditor looks over this information and either gives you credit or denies you credit.

In most cases, you will not receive a report from them on what they used. You will need to order it yourself and check to make sure all the information on it is correct. You can order one free copy of your credit report every year.

The federal government wants you to look at your credit report to make sure it is correct and do so. Expect to do this every year. You are the one who will enjoy making sure that all the information is correct.

Don't forget to do this every year so you can keep up on what is happening with your credit report so you can fix any incorrect information right away.

REVEALING CREDIT SCORE

Today you can check your credit report and credit score much easier than in the past. It was more secretive in the past, but now consumers have more access to the information and this is good. Knowing your credit score will be important to you. Once you understand how your credit score works, you will make changes that can really increase your scores.

BREAKING DOWN THE CREDIT SCORE

Since there are all kinds of different credit scorecards, there is an underlying principal component that all remains the same.

It bases the scores on the same five ingredients, and they are:

1. PAYMENT HISTORY

This is a large part of your credit history. In fact, it is 35% of your score. They base it on your payment history with your creditors, late payments, any types of defaulted accounts, if you have had bankruptcies all have a negative impact on your credit score. The more recent the problem, the greater the damage is to your credit score. Being late on your mortgage one month can drop the amount of your score 120 points using the Mortgage Industry Option scoring model.

It's based on your potential to go 90 days late in the next 2 years. Any recent late payments make them think you will default, and this affects your credit score in a big way. The creditor may not report you unless you are 30 days late, but they can say that you need 10 days to process your payment.

You might have mailed it and you did not think they would report that. The more positive your accounts are, the higher your credit score will be. You should always make sure you pay your bills on time so you can keep your credit score high as it is 35% of the total that makes up your credit score.

2. PERCENTAGE OF HIGH-CREDIT USED

This is what you owe on your higher credit, and it makes up 30% of the total credit score. If you have high credit limits and you are at them, you can almost hurt your credit score as if you were late on your payment. That is because late payments affect 35% of your score. We recommend that clients apply for new credit.

A $5,000 line-of-credit can really help someone to improve their credit score. You will want to apply for one that does not require a credit check and it will give you the credit. Your balances on all of your accounts combined will make a difference. Owing 30% or less on all of your credit card accounts will give you a higher score. Say that you have a $1,000 limit, keep it at $300 or less. For credit cards, you want to keep the smallest balances on them. You want to pay it but not let it go down to $0 because it will not increase the score. You want to keep it at 1%.

Scores will also be because of higher balances on mortgages, car loans, and installment loans. As you pay these types of debts lower, your score will go higher. You can make a tremendous difference in your credit score by opening new accounts and paying them down as agreed. Part of the process is not paying them down to 0 right away. Also, by how many open accounts you have with balances, it will affect your score.

3. THE LENGTH OF YOUR CREDIT HISTORY

This is 15% of your score. The older and the longer you have had credit accounts for, the higher your score will be. Getting more accounts throughout your life and your history will over time grow. You want to be careful how you add credit to your account. Be sure you are checking with all the information before you decide. They can use everything on your credit report and some of it can be damaging.

4. ACCUMULATION OF NEW DEBT

10% of your score comprises your new debt. It depends on how many accounts you have open, how long it has been since you opened one and the request that you have over a 12-month time period. If you have lots of inquiries for a short time period, it will affect your credit score. Too much credit in a short time will really affect your scores badly.

You don't want to apply for a car loan and a home mortgage at the same time because it will look bad. It is also important that you don't let a lot of creditors pull your report at the same time. This also looks terrible and will have an adverse effect on your score.

5. A HEALTHY MIX OF CREDIT ACCOUNTS

This is also 10% of your credit scores. You want to have a healthy mix of them. You may opt to have a mortgage, 3 credit cards, an auto loan, and a few other open accounts. If you have too many, it will lower your score. If you have to open credit card accounts, it makes you look better if you have more or less than 3.

RUNNING INTO PROBLEMS WITH CREDIT

Once again, running into problems with personal credit is a tough time for many people. They feel that their life is over and they cannot do the things they want to. Since this is a very hard time for them, they can talk to family and friends so they will be supportive of their situation while they are going through this tough time.

Since this can affect everything from work to personal relationships, they will want to reach out to those that care about them so they know that they're cared about.

If you find that you are in tough situations, make sure you take the time to reach out and ask for the help that you need. Many family members and friends will be sure to help you when you need it.

They may have also gone through a tough time that required them to do some extraordinary things to get through it. Be sure you are honest about your situation so they can help you in the right way.

23

TAKING ON EXTRA WORK

For many people, taking on extra work is something that they need to do if they run into problems with their finances. They can find extra work in many types of fields. They should make sure that the extra hours that they put in for work will make sense and that it won't interfere with other responsibilities that they have.

Consider this if you need to repair your credit. To improve your score, have that extra money to pay down the debt that you might have so that your score goes up. It is all up to you how you proceed, but most times, this can make an enormous difference in your life. Don't be afraid to try new things so you can add more money to the amount you have so you can get out of debt in a much easier way.

GOOD CREDIT IS THE WAY TO GO

Having good credit is always the best way to go. You want to keep it good at all times. Knowing there might be problems is always a possibility and things happen, so don't give up if you are experiencing them. You will change the situation and work things out so you can live better. If you are younger and you are looking for ways to improve your credit rating and score, you will want to get some accounts you can pay on as agreed.

Make sure that you can afford them. Sit down and make a budget so you know that you can pay off the debts. As you get older, your credit will improve even more and your score will go up higher. You will afford more and spend less than you do so, and this can make all the difference in what you will have and what you will do.

ACCUMULATING DEBT OVER TIME

When you take on more than you can chew, you can have more problems with your credit. You might not think you will ever have a problem, so that is another reason you have to be very careful and make sure you pay your bills every month. You never want to be late because it will have an adverse effect on you. Be sure you work hard all the time so you can pay for the things that you need to.

You will also want to make sure you check your credit report every year. Be sure that the things that are being said about you are true. If they are incorrect, make sure you do something about it so you can have your credit report cleaned and reflect on what is really going on with your financial life. It will surprise you at some mistakes that have shown up on credit reports.

I can't make it more of a point to check it every year for the accuracy that you deserve, so it is reflecting what is really going on with your situation. You'll be glad that you did.

LIVING WITHIN YOUR MEANS

This is hard for some people to do, but you have to learn how to live within your means. Don't spend money on things you don't need and don't go over the budget you have set for yourself. If you are using credit, make sure you use it wisely. If you lose your job, keep looking for another one because it is important to have that income coming in so you can live properly.

Remember that family count and when you need some help, they may be there for you so you can get back on your feet and move on with your life in a better way. It is always a good idea to tell them before a problem arises so they might help you out so you don't get into the trouble that may occur when finances get tough.

A WORD ON BUDGETS

It is so difficult for some people to make out a budget and stick with it.

They need to be patient with themselves and take the time to sit down and write out what they are bringing in and what they have to spend on bills. This will help to keep their expenses in check and make sure they don't run into trouble with their credit.

It is always difficult to bring credit back under control once it has gone bad, but people that stick with their budgets can eventually get it back under the control that they once had. It is always a good idea to write the budget down so you can follow it every month.

This can make all the difference in the world and keep a person from ending up in financial trouble that is too hard for them to get out of.

LEAVE A ONE CLICK REVIEW

Customer Reviews

14,482 Reviews

5 star: (10,243)
4 star: (2,510)
3 star: (702)
2 star: (374)
1 star: (653)

Average Customer Review
★★★★★ (14,482 customer reviews

Most Helpful Customer Reviews

18,653 of 18,810 people found the following review helpful

I'm incredibly over the moon that you're at this point. I would be even more thankful for your feedback.

It will take less than 60 seconds to click and leave a sentence or two for this review!

\>>Click Here and Leave a Review<<

CONCLUSION

Now that you know how to take care of your credit score, do so right away. You are now empowered with the knowledge and tools you need to ensure your new smart personal money credit financial practices can keep you out of BAD debt, obtain and maintain an excellent credit profile and SCORE. Be sure you follow this information so you can keep a healthy credit score to live life in the right way. You will do very well when you keep your personal money credit in good standing by using a SMARTER way.

Your Wealthcome …Leap Forward!

ABOUT THE AUTHOR

DC JAMES is the modern embodiment of the gifted and versatile Renaissance man. Along with being a successful Transformational Life Coach and established Author and Publisher, he is a popular personal Fitness Trainer, Songwriter, Musician, Entrepreneur, and Project and Marketing Consultant.

He began his career in the business sector, a career that had lasted an impressive 25+ years. He has worked for companies like Robert Allen's "Challenge Systems", Upper Deck, Taylor Made Golf, and Watkins Manufacturing.

Very early in his life, he has discovered his talents for helping people maximize their personal and professional growth. He studied life coaching under Dr. Joseph Umidi from LifeFormingCoach.com. DC JAMES specializes in motivating and empowering people to achieve their full potential. His books and tools, such as The A.R.T.F.O.R.M and My LifeZone Journal have inspired and helped many to make a positive change in their lives.

www.ingramcontent.com/pod-product-compliance
Lightning Source LLC
Chambersburg PA
CBHW030516220526
45464CB00006B/2826